Go

At dawn on December 7, 1941, hundreds of bombers, torpedo planes, and fighters, bearing on their fuselages the Rising Sun emblem of the Japanese Empire, took to the air from a great naval carrier task force code-named *Kido Butai*. Their target was the unprepared and unsuspecting U.S. Pacific Fleet anchored at Pearl Harbor in the Hawaiian Islands. This attack, expertly planned and resolutely carried out, was the keystone of a swiftly executed schedule of conquest which would, within six months, bring Japan domination of the entire Far East. It was also an all-but-certain means of national suicide.

To the Japanese in 1941, however, conquest in the Pacific seemed the only way in which their country could solve desperate domestic and international problems. Ever since American Commodore Matthew C. Perry had awakened a slumbering, feudal Japan in 1853, the Mikado's people had made gallant and surprisingly successful efforts to industrialize and win for their country great power status. Yet modernization had stirred civil passions and brought economic and social problems that threatened the very existence of the nation. To solve these problems, Japanese leaders, animated by the warrior spirit of the samurai, planned to carve out a vast new empire in the Orient.

These ambitions, however, collided with American interests and responsibilities in the Far East. For many years the two countries attempted to find some way of creating a balance of power that would preserve peace in the vast Pacific. By 1941 these attempts had utterly failed — and Japan was ready to strike.

PRINCIPALS

HIROHITO — emperor of Japan
FRANKLIN DELANO ROOSEVELT — president of the United States
HIDEKI TOJO — Japanese prime minister
CORDELL HULL — United States secretary of state
ADMIRAL KICHISABURO NOMURA — Japanese ambassador to the United States
JOSEPH C. GREW — United States ambassador to Japan
SABURO KURUSU — Japanese special envoy to the United States
ADMIRAL HUSBAND E. KIMMEL — commander-in-chief, U.S. Pacific Fleet
MAJOR GENERAL WALTER SHORT — United States Army commander in Hawaii
ADMIRAL HAROLD R. STARK — United States chief of naval operations

Remembering Pearl Harbor. A photomontage commemorating the thirtieth anniversary of the Japanese attack on December 7, 1941, shows scenes of twisted masts, blazing ships, a downed enemy plane, and a bewildered sailor comforting a wounded shipmate on Ford Island. At center is memorial to men entombed aboard the U.S.S. Arizona *on that fateful day.*

PEARL HARBOR!

DECEMBER 7, 1941
The Road to Japanese
Aggression in the Pacific

By Robert Goldston

A World Focus Book

FRANKLIN WATTS, INC.
NEW YORK / 1972

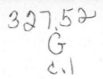

Library of Congress Cataloging in Publication Data

Goldston, Robert C.
    Pearl Harbor! December 7, 1941.
    (A World focus book)

    SUMMARY: A brief history of Japan from 660 B.C. to 1945 with emphasis on the events that led to the attack on Pearl Harbor in 1941.
    Bibliography: p.
    1. U.S.–Foreign relations–Japan–Juvenile literature. 2. Japan–Foreign relations–U.S.–Juvenile literature. 3. Pearl Harbor, Attack on, 1941–Juvenile literature. 4. Japan—History—Juvenile literature. [1. Japan–History. 2. Pearl Harbor, Attack on, 1941. 3. U.S.–Foreign relations–Japan. 4. Japan–Foreign relations–U.S.] I. Title.
E183.8.J3G6   327.52'073   72-1339
ISBN 0-531-02163-7

Contents

Pearl Harbor!

Prologue:
Sunrise in the Pacific

Across the vast expanses of the largest of all the world's oceans the sun rose, of course, at different times. Because of the International Date Line, arbitrarily drawn through the near-empty wastes of the western Pacific, it even came on different days. Thus December 7, 1941, in Washington, D.C., San Francisco, and Hawaii was actually December 8, 1941, in Tokyo, Manila, Singapore, and Hong Kong. Yet in the sense that the westward-sweeping dawn was to open the curtain on one of the greatest conflicts in the history of mankind, one may speak of the sunrise as extending over the entire area of the globe.

Most of the chief actors in the approaching conflict were fully aware that it was about to unfold; but many of them were uncertain as to how, where, and precisely when it would begin. Information regarding Japanese troop and ship movements indicated that Japan was about to attack the British and Dutch colonies in the Far East; but she might simultaneously strike at the American-owned Philippine Islands. Even so, many observers reasoned that while Japan might attack the British (desperately defending themselves in Europe against the onslaught of Hitler's Germany), and the Dutch (already conquered by the Nazi war machine), they would never dare to provoke war against the United States. And, despite the fact that the Japanese had been warned by Washington that any further expansion into Southeast Asia would lead to war, many American leaders, including President Franklin D. Roosevelt, Secretary of State Cordell Hull, and Secretary of War Henry L. Stimson together with their top military advisers, assumed that fighting would be confined to the Far East. Nor had all hopes for peace completely vanished.

3

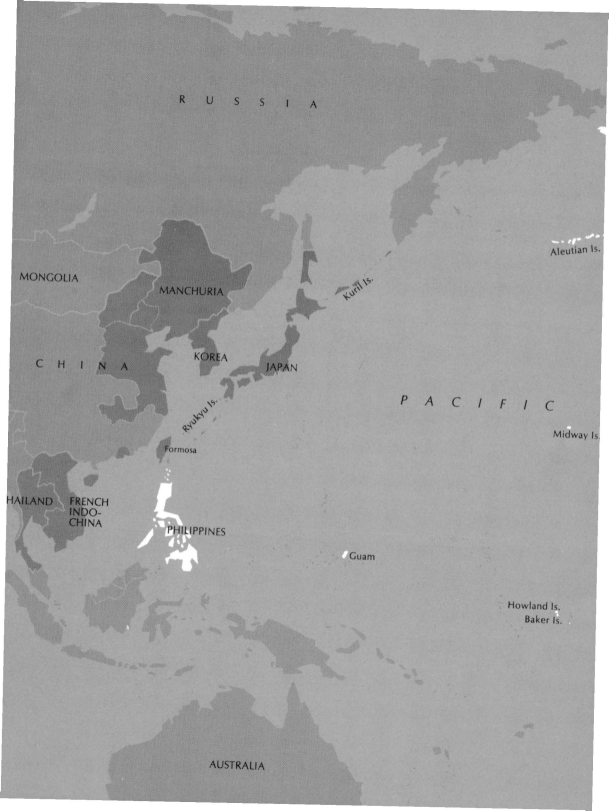

Alaska

THE UNITED STATES

O C E A N

Pearl Harbor

HAWAIIAN ISLANDS

Johnston Is.

THE PACIFIC THEATER, DECEMBER 1941

Japanese expansion

United States expansion

For many months, the Japanese and American governments had been negotiating; mainly through their respective ambassadors, Joseph C. Grew in Tokyo and Admiral Kichisaburo Nomura in Washington. And, as if to emphasize Japan's desire for peace, a special envoy, Saburo Kurusu, had been sent to Washington early in November. But these negotiations had not gone well; in fact, a point of crisis had been reached. President Roosevelt, in a last bid for peace (or at least a delay that would allow the terribly weak American forces in the Pacific to be strengthened), had sent a personal appeal directly to Japanese Emperor Hirohito, reminding him that both nations had "a sacred duty to restore traditional amity and prevent further death and destruction in the world." United States Ambassador Joseph C. Grew delivered this message to the Japanese Foreign Minister Shigenori Togo just after noon on December 7, Washington time.

President Roosevelt's appeal to Emperor Hirohito was not the only message being rushed through diplomatic channels during those hours. The Japanese government had already dispatched a long communication to be delivered by Ambassador Nomura and Special Envoy Kurusu to Secretary of State Cordell Hull. The two Japanese diplomats had been instructed to deliver their message exactly at noon, December 7, Washington time. Neither of them knew why Tokyo attached such great importance to the hour.

Since American military intelligence officers had succeeded in breaking the Japanese secret codes some months before, this message was intercepted, decoded, and presented to President Roosevelt on the evening of December 6. After studying its contents silently, Roosevelt turned to his close friend and special assistant, Harry Hopkins, and said, "This means war."

Japanese Special Envoy Saburo Kurusu (left) and Admiral Kichisaburo Nomura conferring in Washington, D.C.

7

President Franklin D. Roosevelt conferring with Secretary of State Cordell Hull in the anxious days preceding Pearl Harbor.

"Since war is undoubtedly going to come at the convenience of the Japanese," Hopkins remarked, "it's too bad we can't strike the first blow."

"No, we can't do that," Roosevelt replied. "We are a democracy and a peaceful people. But we have a good record."

Then the president attempted to reach Chief of Naval Operations Admiral Harold R. Stark to warn him. But the admiral had gone out to the theater that night, and since Washington had sent many a warning and alert to military bases in the Pacific, it did not seem urgent that yet another be dispatched. The president went to bed.

Not sleeping at all as December 8 (Far Eastern time) dawned were the British, Australian, and Indian soldiers who made up the garrisons of Britain's great Far Eastern fortresses of Singapore and Hong Kong. Since a large Japanese troop convoy had been spotted moving ominously south through the Gulf of Siam, these two bases had been put on full alert. Their defenders were confident because Japanese troops were considered inferior, Singapore was impregnable, and Britain had just sent two of the world's mightiest warships, the battleships *Prince of Wales* and *Repulse,* to reinforce her naval strength in that area.

H.M.S. Prince of Wales, *pride of the Royal Navy, as she appeared early in 1941. This majestic battleship and H.M.S.* Repulse *were both sunk shortly after Pearl Harbor.*

Across the South China Sea, in the Philippines, American and Philippine forces under the command of General Douglas MacArthur were also on the alert. Although it was uncertain that the Japanese would attack there, Major General Lewis H. Brereton, recently arrived commander of MacArthur's Far East Air Force, was taking no chances. The sixteen Flying Fortresses at Clark Field, outside Manila, were lined up on the runways, ready for take-off. There had been frequent reports of unidentified aircraft flying over Philippine airfields for the past few days, and General Brereton did not want his handful of planes caught on the ground in a surprise attack.

December 8 in the Philippines was December 7 in Hawaii — a Sunday. The usual peacetime liberty had been granted to officers and men of the Pacific Fleet anchored in Oahu's Pearl Harbor the night before. Although the Islands' military commanders, Admiral Husband E. Kimmel and Major General Walter Short, were aware of the impending war, they, like their military superiors in Washington, were certain that fighting would break out in the Far East. Nevertheless, a joint army-navy Hawaiian defense plan had been developed to protect the area against submarine attacks and sabotage. But a direct naval or air attack on America's Gibraltar of the Pacific was not to be expected; therefore, only the usual routine air patrols were scheduled for December 7, and the antiaircraft batteries in and around Pearl Harbor were only lightly manned. Most soldiers and sailors on duty in Hawaii would sleep late on a peaceful Sunday morning.

In Tokyo, President Roosevelt's message to the emperor had been dismissed as of little importance by Japanese Prime

General Douglas MacArthur, at the time of Pearl Harbor, was commanding general of U.S. Army Forces in the Far East, which included Philippine troops.

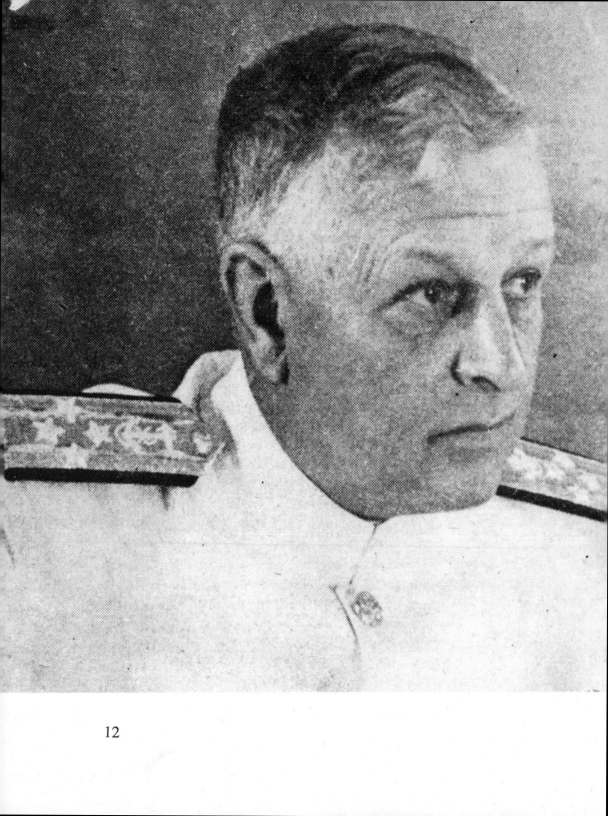

12

Minister Hideki Tojo. "Does it contain any concessions?" he demanded of the foreign minister. When told it did not, he shrugged his shoulders. "It's a pity," he remarked, "to run around disturbing people in the middle of the night." The aide smiled at this comment; its full humor was known to him.

For at that very moment, many thousands of people were about to be disturbed. And while it was true, as American planners surmised, that fighting would break out in the Far East (that big Japanese troop convoy moving through the Gulf of Siam had swung over to the Malayan coast and was even then disembarking thousands of troops to assault British positions ashore), it would not be confined to that area alone.

Japanese planners had decided to gamble their nation's entire future on the striking power of a great naval task force, code-named *Kido Butai*. This awesome assemblage of ships included 2 large battleships, many heavy and light cruisers, and a number of destroyers; but its real striking power was concentrated in 6 aircraft carriers loaded with 81 fighters, 135 dive bombers, 104 regular bombers, and 40 torpedo planes. And *Kido Butai* was not steaming through the Gulf of Siam, the South China Sea, or anywhere else in the Far East where Americans expected the first blow to fall. It was, in fact, now a bare 200 miles northwest of the Hawaiian Islands. *Kido Butai*'s targets were the unsuspecting men and ships of the United States Pacific Fleet anchored in Pearl Harbor.

Admiral Husband E. Kimmel, commander of the U.S. Pacific Fleet when the Japanese made their surprise attack. He and Major General Walter Short, commander of the Hawaiian Department of the Army, were soon relieved of their posts and retired.

In a rolling sea, with only a few clouds to dot an otherwise clear night sky, at 5:45 A.M., Sunday, December 7 (Hawaiian time), the bombers, torpedo planes, and fighters of *Kido Butai* roared down their carrier decks and climbed into formation high above. The first rays of the rising sun lightened the horizon ahead.

Crew members of the Japanese task force code-named Kido Butai *cheer a fighter plane as it roars off the deck of a carrier and heads for Pearl Harbor.*

The Island Nation

If the timing of the Japanese blow at Pearl Harbor, just at dawn, was dictated by sound tactical reasons, to the thousands of officers and men of *Kido Butai* the choice of sunrise as the moment of attack also had a deeply felt symbolic importance. Their homeland, since earliest times, had been known as the Land of The Rising Sun.

For very many centuries — even before the existence of North and South America was suspected — to any Japanese living on one of his nation's more than 3,300 islands, it seemed that Japan was the beginning of the world. To the east, whence rose the sun, there was nothing but thousands of miles of water. To the west, over the narrow seas, commenced the great land mass of Asia; in all the inhabited world the sun rose first over Japan. In fact, the Japanese emperor, according to ancient legend, was a descendant of the Sun Goddess.

The Land of The Rising Sun is a long bow-shaped group of islands arching off the coast of Northeast Asia. From its northern extremity to its southern, this bow of islands covers about 1,000 miles. Most of its inhabitants (in 1941 these numbered more than 73,000,000) live on the four largest islands, Hokkaido, Honshu, Kyushu, and Shikoku, and almost all live within the shadow of mountains. In fact, Japan is primarily a spine of mountains rising out of the sea. Many of the peaks are volcanic and the entire mass rests on a zone of earth-crust instability; minor earthquakes are daily affairs, major ones occur on an average of every six years. So mountainous is the nation that a bare 15 percent of its land area is suitable for agriculture. When it is realized that this land area *as a whole* barely approximates that of the state of California while Japan's population is about half that

15

of the entire United States, it will be seen that simply feeding Japan's crowded millions has been a grave problem for many years. Despite the fact that the Japanese also farm the sea, Japan must import food or starve.

To an island people, of course, the sea is a central element in life, myth, and history. The earliest inhabitants of Japan probably came across the narrow seas from Asia. They came at different times and from different places so that the Japanese people are really composed of several different races although they are now relatively homogeneous. This settlement occurred thousands of years before recorded history. Indeed, history in Japan remained largely myth and legend until as late as A.D. 700 when it began to be recorded in Chinese script, which was adopted as Japan's official bureaucratic language.

According to ancient legends, the first human (as opposed to divine) emperor was Jimmu Tenno, who supposedly reigned some 650 years before the Christian era. He was a warrior and a direct descendant of the Sun Goddess. With his rule begins a very long and very complex reign of emperors and imperial families, all claiming descent from Jimmu Tenno. At first these emperors ruled only over certain areas of the main islands; they had to battle opposing clans and the "barbarian" Ainus who inhabited the northern islands to extend their dominions. Sometimes there were two powerful leaders, each claiming sovereignty. The imperial capital was moved from place to place with alarming frequency; in fact, the building of new palaces became a very severe burden on the peasantry. Periods of relative stability alternated with periods of civil upheavals and war. The lot of the masses — peasants and fishermen — was rarely a happy one. But from this welter of dynasties, wars, and imperial rivalries, certain themes and salient facts are worth noting.

16

According to ancient Japanese legends, the emperor Jimmu, a direct descendant of the Sun Deity, became the first human monarch of Japan. Here, after subjugating rebellious chieftains, Jimmu sets up an altar to worship the gods of heaven and earth.

Of very great importance was the prehistoric establishment of Shinto as the state religion. Basically, Shinto derived from the worship of the pagan Sun God and Goddesses as well as the forces of nature in their various godlike embodiments. By historical times, however, it had grown into an elaborate rite of ancestor worship. Since the emperor was supposedly the lineal descendant of the Sun Goddess, this meant that he was actually a god himself, to be worshiped and blindly obeyed by every Japanese. Many of the emperors were warrior kings and certain of their knightly soldiers (the *samurai*) later developed a code of behavior (*Bushido*) that bound them to serve the emperor until death. Suicide was preferable to either surrender or failure in the service of the god-emperor. The elaborate suicide rite, commonly called *hara-kiri,* came into existence as a way of atoning to the emperor (and hence to heaven) for failure in one's cause.

Because the mountains made communications (except by sea) difficult and uncertain between various regions, and because of the cult of ancestor worship, the power of the family unit as a local governing agency grew to very important proportions in Japan. Each major clan felt itself in control of its locality; and, while reverence was paid to the emperor (along with taxes and military service), too much imperial interference in local affairs could provoke war between the more powerful clans and the central government. Aside from that, the clans fought each other almost constantly. This geopolitical chaos gave rise in Japan, as it did in medieval Europe, to a feudal system of government with local lords supreme over their own territory and serfs, owing allegiance to a hierarchy of nobles that culminated in the emperor himself.

18

Another factor of great weight in Japanese history was the cultural dependence of Japan upon the older and much more sophisticated civilization of neighboring China. Trade and diplomatic relations between these two countries reached back to legendary times. While the emperor of China considered himself the overlord of the emperor of Japan (as indeed he did of most neighboring countries), the intervening seas saved Japan from complete subjugation to the Celestial Empire, although hostilities occurred more than a few times between them. The last great Chinese attempt to conquer Japan was undertaken by Kublai Khan, the Mongol ruler, during the thirteenth century A.D. His forces were repulsed and his huge invasion fleet destroyed by a providential typhoon. Nonetheless, Chinese customs, inventions, art, and learning were eagerly copied by the Japanese over the centuries. In the eighth century A.D., as we have seen, Chinese script was adopted as Japan's official language. Even earlier, in the sixth century A.D., the Buddhist religion was imported from China and soon flourished in Japan. The teachings of the great Chinese sage Confucius formed the basis of one of the earliest Japanese law codes. Japanese missions to China, sent with the express purpose of learning and copying whatever was new and useful, continued into the ninth century.

In the ninth century A.D., in yet another of the almost constant wars between the imperial government and the Ainu people of the north, a noble named Sakanoue Tamuramaro so distinguished himself in the fighting that he was granted the title of *Sei-i-tai-Shogun,* or the barbarian-subduing-generalissimo. This title of shogun later became very important, for although the emperors continued to be revered, and from time to time even displayed the capacity to rule, more and more real power was

concentrated in the hands of the shogun. Like the imperial crown itself, the title of shogun was hereditary within the most powerful families until it was wrested from them by some other powerful family. Eventually the shogunate, combining the functions of prime minister, war leader, and many other offices, became the actual ruling force in Japan, with the emperors no more than titular heads of the nation.

Finally, a factor of the greatest importance in Japanese history was that of continued isolation until comparatively recent times. Like China and Korea, Japan had no contact with European civilization and but little with that of the rest of Asia. Moreover, Japan's geographical position in the northwest Pacific ensured the nation that it was able to maintain its isolation long after China had been forcibly "opened" by Western powers. Thus many of the elements of Japanese history were "frozen" into a way of life undisturbed until the middle of the nineteenth century. When Japan finally entered upon the stage of modern history, it was as a nation in which nothing essential had changed for a thousand years.

The first contact between Japan and Europe came in 1542 when a Portuguese ship took shelter in the harbor of a small island at the southern tip of Kyushu. The ship was well received, and when news of the event spread to other Portuguese trading posts in the Orient, no less than seven expeditions were dispatched to carry on trade with Japan. In 1549 one of these expeditions brought a Jesuit priest, Francis Xavier, who spent two years in Japan attempting to spread the Christian gospel.

A portrait of the great Chinese sage Confucius. His teachings formed the basis for one of the earliest Japanese law codes.

Although his visit resulted in only 760 conversions, he is credited with being the founder of Japanese Christianity, for his efforts, and those of other Jesuit priests, bore an astonishing harvest. Within thirty years there were more than 150,000 converts, and by A.D. 1600 there were more than 300,000. Yet the very success of Christianity was to prove that religion's undoing.

While the Japanese welcomed trade with the Portuguese and later the Spaniards when they inherited Portugal's eastern empire, and were eager to learn all they could about European civilization, Japan's social structure proved too rigid to accommodate much of what they learned. The feudal lords of Japan (some of whom were themselves converted) suspected — quite rightly — that Christianity would prove a subversive doctrine among their long-suffering serfs. Also, they noted that rival Christian sects did not hesitate to revile each other in a most un-Christian fashion. Perhaps of decisive importance was the slow realization that Christianity might well be a political weapon to prepare the way for conquest. The Catholic missionaries had boasted of how their work had helped the King of Spain conquer the Indian empires of the New World; and Japanese travelers brought back tales of how European trading stations in India, China, and other Far Eastern areas had a way of developing into bases for conquest. Finally, the Christians in Japan became involved in the bloody rivalries of the feudal clans and the shoguns.

From 1614 to 1639, the Japanese feudal lords and shoguns adopted an ever stricter policy against Christianity. Violence flared during which many priests were beheaded; Japanese Chris-

The Jesuit priest Francis Xavier is credited with being the founder of Christianity in Japan.

tians were forced to recant their faith on pain of death. In 1637 Japanese Christians near the town of Nagasaki rose in revolt against the shogunate, but were subdued in an appalling massacre — more than 37,000 being put to the sword. Imperial edicts forbade any Japanese to go abroad, expelled all Spaniards and Portuguese from the nation, and even forbade the construction of ships large enough to cross the oceans. Henceforth, Portuguese and Spanish ships touched at Japan only at their own risk — more than one unlucky vessel was burned and its crew executed.

Thus Japan was effectively sealed off once again from outsiders. But in this there was one exception. Dutch merchants had arrived in Japan in 1600. Perhaps because they were able to convince the Japanese that Protestant Holland was the archenemy of Catholic Spain, perhaps because Dutch vessels helped in the suppression of the Christians near Nagasaki, perhaps because the Dutch attempted no missionary work, they alone of the nations of Europe were allowed to maintain a tiny trading post on an artificial island in the harbor at Nagasaki. For the next two hundred years they were the only "foreigners" allowed any contact at all with Japan.

But if Japan desired isolation from the rest of the world, the spread of commerce and the power of the industrialization of Europe made that desire hopeless. The might of English naval power was impressed upon the Japanese when they learned of how England had defeated the mighty Chinese empire and forced the conquered Chinese into unfavorable trade agreements. When China ceded Hong Kong to the British, it was apparent that archaic military force could not stand up against modern weaponry. Eventually, Japan would have to adopt Western ways or succumb, as had China, to Western imperialism. But the Japanese remained cautious. In 1842 the shogun instructed local feudal lords that foreign ships were no longer to be seized nor their crews put to death. Later it was allowed that foreign vessels driven by storms into Japanese waters were to be permitted to buy necessary food and supplies. Meanwhile, the growth of the whaling industry had brought not only European, but also American ships to the waters of the northwest Pacific. When they were occasionally forced into Japanese harbors, their welcome was inhospitable, to say the least. Despite the shogun's instructions, feudal lords were fond of bombarding these ships whenever they came within range.

To attempt to remedy this situation, the United States Congress passed a resolution in 1845 that urged commercial relations be established with Japan. Accordingly, in the following year, Commodore James Biddle and two United States naval vessels visited the Japanese port of Uraga. Biddle stayed nine days. Not only were his attempts to contact Japanese officials rebuffed, but he and his men were very roughly handled by soldiers of the local feudal lord. Under orders not to offer violence, Commodore Biddle sailed away, his mission a failure.

The American government was determined to persevere, and on July 8, 1853, Commodore Matthew C. Perry anchored four powerful warships in Uraga Harbor. He bore a letter from President Millard Fillmore to the emperor requesting the conclusion of a commercial treaty. Unlike his predecessors of various nationalities, Commodore Perry had spent months studying everything he could find on Japan. He understood the great importance of ritual and dignity in the Japanese social structure. When local officials objected that the emperor was too august a personage to receive the commodore, Perry, styling himself "The Lord of The Forbidden Interior," made clear that his own dignity demanded that he either meet with a member of the imperial fam-

Commodore Matthew Perry meeting the imperial commissioners of Japan.

ily itself or die (as would a samurai) in attempting to deliver the letter personally. Impressed both by Perry's impeccable behavior and by the armament of his naval vessels, the Japanese negotiators finally brought forward a prince of the royal family to whom Perry delivered the president's message. After distributing gifts to his hosts, the commodore sailed away, remarking that he would return for an answer.

The Japanese, who, since the days of the Mongol invasion, had never seen more than two foreign naval vessels together, were panic stricken at the obvious power of the American squadron. The emperor himself was informed of the awesome event and he ordered that prayers for the destruction of the foreign barbarians should be offered at the seven principal shrines of Japan.

These prayers were of no avail. Commodore Perry returned in February 1854 with an even more powerful squadron — ten ships and 2,000 men. After six weeks of negotiations he obtained a treaty of peace and friendship which stipulated that the Japanese ports of Shimoda and Hakodate should be opened to United States trading vessels, that shipwrecked sailors should obtain relief in Japanese waters, and that a United States consular agent should reside in Shimoda.

Perry stayed in Japan until June 1854, when he sailed away to Canton, China. Behind him he left a feudal nation suddenly brought face-to-face with the modern world. He also left behind him a nation in deep ferment, on the verge of revolutionary changes which, within the space of a generation, were utterly to transform a thousand-year-old society.

The Making of Modern Japan

Even before the arrival of Commodore Perry, the ancient and creaking political system by which Japan was ruled had shown signs of degeneration. The shogunate had fallen into the hands of incompetent men, the emperor remained isolated from real power, and the great feudal chieftains showed less and less inclination to heed the commands of the central government. The arrival of foreigners only intensified and complicated the central Japanese problem of establishing a unified government.

The feudal chiefs, suspicious of Western influences that might eventually undermine their privileged economic and social position, took the lead in arousing and manipulating antiforeign sentiment. Fear and hatred of the "barbarians" was associated with a whipped-up reverence for the emperor. After all, it had been agents of the shogun, not of the emperor, who had acceded to the demands of the hated foreigners. Soon antiforeign and superpatriotic sentiment was coupled with an increasing demand that the emperor resume his real powers and authority and abolish the shogunate. That this would serve further to enhance the independent power of the feudal chieftains to the detriment of unified government was a fact that escaped the masses of Japanese peasants. As it happened, the feudal chieftains themselves were deeply mistaken.

Inevitably this antiforeign frenzy led to murderous attacks upon Europeans in Japan. Furthermore, individual feudal chieftains once again took to bombarding foreign trading vessels that wandered within the range of their cannon. The fact that the shogun had concluded commercial and diplomatic treaties with England (1859) and France (1860) modeled on the treaty previously concluded with the United States was of no interest to the semi-independent and rebellious feudal lords. These incidents led to the bombardment by a British fleet of the town of Kagoshima in August 1863, and later, in 1864, to the bombardment of Shimonoseki by a combined squadron of British, French, Dutch, and American warships.

The bombardment of Shimonoseki in 1864 by the combined squadron of French, British, and Dutch warships.

It might be supposed that all this would have served to strengthen the influence of the shogun, who had all along insisted on the necessity of dealing amicably with the Western powers. But it did not. It simply made several things very clear. Firstly, it underscored the fact that Japan could no longer afford two governments — either the shogun or the emperor would have to go. Secondly, it highlighted the fact that the feudal chieftains would absolutely have to be brought under the authority of one central government. Thirdly, it made perfectly obvious the fact that unless Japan industrialized quickly, she would fall prey to Western imperialism. That Japan must modernize, that she needed one central government, that the power of the feudal chieftains must be broken — all of this was certain. And in choosing between government by the shogun and government by the emperor, the outcome could not be in doubt. The abolition of the emperor was unthinkable to any Japanese — it would be the shogunate that would go.

This political crisis coincided with the accession to the imperial throne in 1867 of a very remarkable ruler — Mutsuhito. Mutsuhito took the name of Meiji (meaning "Enlightened Government") and one of his first official acts was to accept the resignation of the last shogun. In Japanese history, the abolition of the shogunate and the reemergence of the emperor as the true ruling authority throughout the nation is called the Restoration — and it inaugurated a time of rapid change. Between 1868 and 1876 the entire structure of feudalism in Japan was abolished. The great feudal chieftains surrendered their lands and holdings to the imperial government, serfdom was abolished, taxation be-

The emperor Meiji (Mutsuhito).

came the sole prerogative of the central government, the warrior samurai class was invited to give up its special status, a national army was formed, and a conscription law was passed making every adult male, regardless of his social standing, liable to military service.

All of this was accomplished with amazingly little opposition. It might be supposed that the feudal chieftains would fight for their ancient rights to the last inch. Quite to the contrary, the most powerful among them voluntarily accepted the imperial rescripts and joined the new government ministry established by Emperor Meiji. They were equally docile in surrendering their rights to impose taxation and their feudal powers over lesser nobles and serfs. Even more surprising was the resignation with which the samurai accepted their loss of status. There were no less than 400,000 samurai in Japan at that time; had they banded together to fight for their ancient privileges they could easily have seized control of the government. That they did not was due to their reverence for the emperor.

The abolition of feudalism did produce one serious reactionary uprising, the Satsuma Rebellion. Partly due to the wounded feelings of certain samurai, partly to the ambitions of a powerful family, and partly to the superpatriotic folly of certain government ministers who were angered that the emperor's cabinet refused to reply to Korean insults with a declaration of war, the clan in control of Satsuma province rose in rebellion in 1877. The rebels put 40,000 well-trained men in the field but they were soon defeated by the new national army. This demonstrated to all Japanese that military virtue was not the sole prerogative of the samurai class and, since the rebels found no support whatsoever outside their own district, that resistance to the new order was but an isolated phenomenon.

But if the feudal chieftains and samurai by and large acceded gracefully to these fundamental changes, what of the masses of peasants? The docility and discipline that had been instilled in them by untold centuries of subservience to emperor and noble along with the reforms undertaken by the new regime led them to welcome the modernization of Japan enthusiastically. Just as the nation had adopted Chinese culture in the eighth century, welcomed European Christianity in the sixteenth, driven the Europeans out and "closed" Japan in the seventeenth, they accepted the inevitability of change in the nineteenth with astonishing equanimity. They were to show the same spirit of obedient conformity in accepting both war and defeat in the twentieth century.

In the years following the Satsuma Rebellion, the imperial government literally legislated Japan into the modern world. All restrictions on Japanese intercourse with the outside world were removed; Christianity and other foreign religions were permitted; a postal system, a system of public schools, and an independent press were established. Industry was encouraged with liberal government grants and tax rebates and European and American models were eagerly copied. Japan's first railway (between Tokyo and Yokohama) was built with the assistance of English engineers and opened in 1872. Harbors were modernized and the foundations of a great merchant marine were laid. Thousands of young Japanese were sent abroad to study at government expense.

How willing the Japanese were to copy what they considered to be the best of the Western models was demonstrated by the fact that the new criminal code of laws (1882) was modeled on that of France; civil and commercial codes (1899) followed German examples; and the first constitution, when it was promulgated in 1889, was based on English, German, and American experience.

The establishment of representative government in Japan was a stormy question that created endless difficulties for decades. Although the imperial government had promised a constitution in 1881, it seemed reluctant to proceed. There were, in fact, many obstacles. First of all, the imperial government feared that a representative assembly would fall under the control of one or another of the powerful clans, for although the feudal chieftains had been stripped of their feudal rights, they remained the richest and most powerful men in the nation. It was their money that now flowed to establish industry; it was they who really controlled their local districts. The political parties that were just coming into existence during the last decades of the nineteenth century were really hardly more than political expressions of the power of certain clans. Establishing a representative government might simply be opening the way to the reemergence of a shogunate. Nor did the fact that the new opposition parties used political assassination as one of their chief weapons reassure the imperial government.

Nevertheless, a new constitution was devised that provided for two chambers more or less like the English Parliament. The House of Peers included all princes and marquises, 20 percent of all remaining peers elected by themselves, citizen delegates nominated by the fifteen richest men in Japan, and certain men of learning and wisdom nominated by the emperor himself. The House of Representatives (which had the right to legislate, impose taxes, and petition the emperor) was to consist of three hundred members elected by adult males who payed at least fifteen yen (a not inconsiderable sum of money in those days) in direct taxes. A cabinet system with a prime minister appointed

34

by the emperor but also responsible to the parliament was established.

While postal systems may be established by imperial edict and factories built by steel and engineers, the formation of a democratic and representative government is not something that can be effected overnight. The system of government in England and the United States had grown painfully and slowly and was accompanied by the establishment of the common law and the growth of political responsibility and practice among their peoples. In Japan no such development had ever taken place. Japan had always been ruled by arbitrary force; it was unrealistic to suppose that the ingrained customs of more than a thousand years could be swept away in a decade. The fears that parliament would fall under the control of certain clans proved well-founded — but the corruption of the Japanese political system was not fundamental. What was fundamental was the fact that Japan continued to be ruled by cliques of the richest and most powerful men who, with the emperor's consent, could pass any law, embark on any war, enforce whatever rules they chose. To the vast masses of the Japanese people the emperor's word remained the word of God. And, although any governmental decree signed by the imperial hand had the effect of a divine order, with the introduction of the new system of government, the emperor was morally (and sometimes legally, as was the king of England) bound to accept the advice of his cabinet.

Of course this could work both ways. If a truly liberal and democratic administration should come to power, its orders would also be unhesitatingly obeyed. But the restrictions upon voting, the structure of the new government, the economic and local political power of the old clans, the traditional martial spirit of the ruling class, and the ignorance of masses of people totally unused to self-rule all but assured that only the most conservative and reactionary administrations would come to power.

If the creation of a new governmental structure presented problems, the establishment of a modern army and navy did not. All Japanese, very much aware of the fate of other Asiatic nations at the hands of Western imperialists, eagerly supported and uncomplainingly payed increased taxes to achieve military security. Arsenals and naval dockyards were established; modern weapons based on European models were manufactured; German, French, and English officers were invited to help train the new Japanese army in their use; and naval vessels were purchased from England until Japan was able to produce her own.

The rapidity and dedication with which Japan created a modern army and navy were amply demonstrated in 1894 when war broke out with China. At issue between the two nations was an ancient bone of contention; the status of the Kingdom of Korea. China, from time immemorial, had claimed that Korea was a vassal state, autonomous, but owing allegiance to the Chinese emperor. Its proximity to Japan had, also since time immemorial, made it a natural area for Japanese trade, investment, and economic exploitation. Domestic affairs in Korea were in a constant state of turmoil; so weak was the Korean government that it seemed inevitable that sooner or later the country would fall into the hands of one or more of the European imperialist powers. The Koreans, hating the Chinese and Japanese equally, made life dangerous in their nation for the citizens of both countries. For this reason both Japanese and Chinese troops were sometimes stationed in Korean cities.

In 1894 a native rebellion against the Korean government broke out (such uprisings were frequent) and China dispatched troops, describing Korea as a "tributary state" of the Chinese

The Japanese attack at Song-Hwan, Korea, 1894.

empire. Japan, suspicious of this move, responded by sending more troops of her own, and demanding of China that if Korea was really a "tributary state" then order and peace must be restored. When the rebellion died a natural death, Japan informed China that any further reinforcement of the Chinese garrisons already in Korea would be considered a hostile and aggressive act.

The Chinese replied by dispatching a convoy of 1,200 men. This convoy ran into the Japanese cruiser *Naniwa* and was sunk. War was declared a few days later (August 1, 1894), and Japan had a chance to test her new army and navy. The test was a triumphant success. Japanese troops swept everything before them in Korea, and Japanese squadrons sank every flotilla the Chinese sent against them. On April 17, 1895, China admitted defeat when, by the Treaty of Shimonoseki, it acknowledged Korean independence and ceded to Japan the large island of Formosa, the Pescadores Islands, and control of portions of the southern half of Manchuria. But Japanese elation over this victory was soured when Russia, Germany, and France demanded that Japan not occupy Manchuria permanently — and backed up their demand with the threat of war. Japan backed down in the face of this European threat and redoubled her efforts to achieve a military capability that in the future would enable her to defy such foreign interference.

Japanese ambitions in Asia now ran head-on into the imperialistic designs of tsarist Russia. While the Japanese were attempting to exploit their new position in Korea, Russian influence kept that country in a state of defiance against Japan. Likewise

Admiral Heihachiro Togo, under whose command the Imperial Japanese Fleet sank most of the Russian Baltic Fleet during the Russo-Japanese War of 1904–5.

the Russians, exploiting Chinese weaknesses, extended their influence into Manchuria. Using the Chinese Boxer Rebellion as a pretext, the Russians sent troops to occupy Manchuria and then refused to withdraw them after the rebellion had been suppressed. When Japan sent a team of diplomats to St. Petersburg to negotiate a solution to the problem of Russo-Japanese rivalry in the Far East, the Russians refused to talk seriously and treated the Japanese mission with contempt. Accordingly, Japan broke off diplomatic relations with Russia on February 6, 1904. War seemed inevitable.

Japan's declaration of war on Russia in 1904 took the form of a surprise attack on the Russian Far Eastern Squadron at anchor in Port Arthur. The Japanese Fleet, composed mostly of English-built battleships and cruisers, led by Admiral Heihachiro Togo, bombarded the Russian fleet on the night of February 8-9 and sank most of it. When, in the following year, the Russians sent their Baltic Fleet around the world to the Sea of Japan, Admiral Togo utterly destroyed it in the great naval battle of Tsushima.

Japanese success at sea was matched by Japanese victories on land; the great Russian Far Eastern strongholds of Port Arthur and Harbin finally fell after offering tough resistance. The pressures of the war, combined with the imperialistic aims and ineffective leadership, led to uprisings in Russia (and, eventually, the Revolution of 1905), while in Japan the mounting cost in men and money was becoming a severe strain. Both sides were eager, therefore, to accept the invitation of American President Theodore Roosevelt to mediate the struggle.

In the peace treaty signed between Russia and Japan at Portsmouth, New Hampshire, on September 5, 1905, Japan won recognition of her "paramount interests" in Korea, the evacua-

Cartoon shows President Theodore Roosevelt mediating between Russia and Japan at Portsmouth, New Hampshire. A treaty of peace was signed there on September 5, 1905.

41

tion of all foreign troops from Manchuria (except Japanese railway guards), Russia's lease on Port Arthur and the southern section of the Russian-built Manchurian railway, and the southern half of Russia's Sakhalin Island. But because the Russians were not required to pay an indemnity, the treaty of Portsmouth was so unpopular in Japan that rioting broke out in Tokyo. Nevertheless the Japanese had won more than territory and economic interests in their successful war against tsarist Russia. With all the nations of the world watching attentively, they had demonstrated that an Oriental nation could defeat a European power. In fact, they had won for themselves recognition as one of the world's great powers and a force to be reckoned with in the Far East and the Pacific.

The Pacific Time Bomb

When the Venetian traveler Marco Polo made his long journey to the splendid court of Kublai Khan in China late in the thirteenth century, the Orient was incomparably more prosperous, civilized, and powerful than Europe. Compared to the Chinese empire, to the great Mogul empire of India, or to the central Asiatic strongholds of the Mongols, the petty states of feudal Europe were "underdeveloped" nations. In fact the hordes of the Mongols had conquered Europe as far as the gates of Vienna against but weak resistance — and had it not been for internal dissension among them, the Mongol warriors might well have swept on to the Atlantic.

Six hundred years later, however, the situation was reversed. Having long since shaken off feudalism, having passed through ages of revolution, discovery, and scientific advance, by the beginning of the nineteenth century Europe had emerged as the dominant continent in the world. While the old Oriental empires stagnated, Europe, through industrialization, developed muscles of steel. And with these muscles she embarked on an era of imperialistic exploitation in the Americas, Africa, and Asia. Whereas Europeans had previously met with only semibarbaric Indian civilizations in Mexico and South America, the resistance of savage Indian tribes in North America, and the desolate ruins of once-mighty black civilizations in Africa, they encountered in Asia cultures which, if weak in terms of modern industry, were ancient, continuous, and in many respects more highly developed than their own.

When, during the eighteenth century, it became fully apparent that European trade and missionary work were but the prelude to European domination, conquest, and colonialization, the people of the old civilizations of Asia attempted to fight off the "foreign barbarians." In this they were hampered not only by their lack of industry, but also by patterns of religion, political structure, and philosophy unsuited to an industrial-scientific age. If it is true, as one observer has pointed out, that "gunboats bring their own philosophy," then there was very little in Oriental culture that could cope with the brute power of the Western imperialists.

Since communications with the Orient were primarily by sea, that European nation which controlled the seas would inevitably lead the way in exploiting the great resources and markets of the East. Each in their turn, the Portuguese lost their supremacy to the Spaniards, the Spaniards to the Dutch, and the Dutch to the English. During the eighteenth and early nineteenth centuries, English sea power made that nation supreme upon the world's trade routes and won for it control of the rimlands of the Arabian peninsula, the Indian Ocean islands, and the great subcontinent of India itself. From India, English trade and, inevitably, English power, expanded into the Chinese empire. When England's East India Company found that the opium it grew in India could be sold at great profit to China, England did not hesitate to wage war on the Celestial Empire to ensure a continuing market for the drug.

Although England's position was dominant east of Suez, it was not exclusive. During the middle of the nineteenth century, France seized the valuable area of Southeast Asia that she called French Indochina. The Dutch retained their ancient hold upon the Dutch East Indies, as did Spain upon the Philippine Islands. After the creation of the German empire in 1870, that nation,

44

too, secured a toehold on the Asiatic coast in the form of a forced lease of a Chinese peninsula. Meantime, tsarist Russia, expanding ever eastward into the vastness of Siberia, finally established itself, as we have seen, on the Sea of Japan, and attempted to extend its power into Manchuria and Korea.

During the latter half of the nineteenth century it seemed probable that all of China might be carved up into colonies by the great European powers. The weak and despised Manchu dynasty that ruled that vast nation could offer no effective resistance. Europeans in the great coastal ports lived in their own enclaves in which they enforced their own law; European warships patrolled Chinese rivers, and any resistance to these incursions was answered by a European expeditionary force being dispatched to ravage the countryside and the inland cities. The imperial capital at Peking was occupied several times by English and French forces. Probably the only thing that saved China from colonization was the fact that the European nations suspected each other's motives — any exaggerated claim by one of them would be resisted by the others. As it became apparent that rivalry over the spoils of Asia might lead to war in Europe, the Western powers moved more cautiously.

The European imperialist powers were joined, in 1898, by the United States. With the closing of the western frontier and the establishment of real American power on the shores of the Pacific, American eyes naturally looked westward to the riches of the lands beyond the Pacific horizon. American expansionism found a victim in the decayed power of Spain, an excuse in the endless and bloody rebellions of Cubans against their Spanish overlords, and a new weapon in the rebirth of a powerful American navy. But if the Spanish-American War of 1898 was sup-

45

posedly fought to "free Cuba," it really resulted in the transfer of Spain's great Pacific colony of the Philippines to American control. When the United States Asiatic Squadron under Admiral Dewey sank the Spanish Far Eastern Squadron in Manila Bay on May 1, 1898, the United States emerged as another imperialist power in Asia — with vital interests to protect there.

And when, after three years of bloody guerrilla warfare, American troops finally suppressed the Philippine Independence Movement led by Emilio Aguinaldo, it seemed that the United States was prepared to take its fair share of the spoils of the Orient. To ensure that Americans would not be excluded from the plunder of China, United States Secretary of State John Hay sent a note to the European powers requesting them to maintain an "open door," for the trade of all nations in China. When Chinese exasperation led to the Boxer Rebellion of 1899–1900, American troops joined those of England, France, Germany, and Japan in crushing the rebels and occupying the Chinese capital of Peking. Now American forces were stationed in the Chinese coastal ports and American gunboats patrolled Chinese rivers.

As has been seen, one of the decisive influences in the opening and industrialization of Japan had been Japanese fears of falling prey, like the other nations of Asia, to Western imperialism. While the Japanese maintained an attitude of correct neutrality toward the American conquest of the Philippines (and the annexation of the Hawaiian Islands, Guam, and Wake Island), her leaders did not welcome the replacement of a decayed and inefficient Spanish presence by that of a dynamic and powerful

A portrait of Admiral George Dewey, under whose command the U.S. Asiatic Squadron destroyed the Spanish Far Eastern Squadron at Manila Bay in May 1898.

American one. And when Spain, having lost her greatest Far Eastern colony, sold the vast island chains of the Marshalls, the Carolines, and the Marianas to imperial Germany, Japanese suspicions were by no means allayed. But meantime, events closer to home commanded Japanese attention.

The Japanese fruits of victory in her war against Russia in 1905 had included recognition of her "paramount political, military and economic interests" in Korea. This presupposed that Japan could maintain these interests in the face of Korean resistance, and also that the other European powers would accept Japanese domination of Korea. England, feeling the first chill winds of the twentieth century, and suddenly aware that she might one day need allies in the Far East, concluded the Anglo-Japanese Alliance in 1902. By its terms, the Japanese position in Korea was recognized and both nations promised to come to each other's aid in case either was attacked by a third. Other treaties were concluded in 1907 with France and Russia that further consolidated Japanese power in Korea. By 1910 the Japanese felt secure enough in their occupation of that strife-torn country to annex it outright to the Japanese empire.

Although relations between the United States and Japan had generally been good, it was, at a very early date, quite apparent to American military and political leaders that the most natural threat to American possession of the Philippine Islands would be Japanese expansionism. The Japanese were firmly established in the nearby Pescadores Islands and in the great bastion of Formosa that they had won from China. As early as the turn of the century, American naval staffs had been wondering how they would defend the Philippines should Japan choose to strike.

President Theodore Roosevelt, himself an aggressive expansionist, had expressed his worry over how the United States could protect American interests in Asia unless the nation was prepared to one day wage an all-out war. It was extremely doubtful that American public opinion would support a full-scale war in Asia in defense of obscure treaty rights in China or Manchuria or to protest Japanese expansion in Korea. Moreover, it was not altogether certain that Americans would enthusiastically go to war to protect the United States position in the Philippines. But with expanded American responsibilities and interests, the Roosevelt and later administrations undertook to build a huge American fleet — one powerful enough to fight in both the Atlantic and the Pacific if necessary. And to ensure the quick transfer of fleet units from one ocean to the other, territory was seized in Central America and the Panama Canal was dug.

The first faint flickerings of lightning in Japanese-American relations came early in the twentieth century. In 1906, the California State Legislature, in a fever of racism and prejudice, passed a resolution urging the Federal Government to exclude any further Japanese immigration into their state. Furthermore, the city of San Francisco decreed that Japanese children would have to attend separate schools. Although there were only about 65,000 Japanese residents in California at the time, the Japanese government and people quite rightly felt deeply insulted by these actions. President Theodore Roosevelt attempted to influence the Californians, and the offensive legislation was withdrawn in 1907. But it was not easy for him to explain to Japanese diplomats how, under the American federal system of government, such actions could take place locally.

A few months later, in 1908, President Roosevelt dispatched

The "Great White Fleet" as it left the Virginia Capes for its "show the
flag" world cruise. U.S.S. Connecticut heads the column of battleships.

50

the new American navy on a round-the-world tour. The so-called "Great White Fleet" was intended to dazzle America's friends and discourage her enemies by its show of strength. Just as the California crisis was being settled, it was heading to the Pacific (by way of Cape Horn, the Panama Canal not yet being in existence). Not a few European powers expected war to break out between the United States and Japan as soon as the fleet reached Eastern waters.

As it turned out, common sense prevailed on both sides. The hateful and illegal "Japanese Exclusion Acts" of California had been repealed and the Japanese concluded an agreement (known as the "Gentleman's Agreement") with the United States to limit Japanese emigration to America. The Japanese government sincerely lived up to this pact and, when the Great White Fleet arried in Tokyo Bay, it was greeted enthusiastically. In fact, according to its commander, Admiral ("Fighting Bob") Evans, the fleet's reception in Japan was the friendliest it received anywhere.

Yet the pressures upon Japan to continue its Asiatic expansion did not lessen. The modernization of the country had caused (due to better medical care) a great increase in population; while emigration might relieve some of the pressure, it could by no means solve Japan's basic problem of trying to feed too many people from too little land. Likewise, the industrialization of Japan, although it provided the export profits with which Japan might buy food abroad, created new demands — both for raw materials (of which Japan had practically none) and for new markets. In the Japanese view there was a vital difference between her need for export markets and the needs of other nations.

While the income derived from exports might strengthen the economy of the United States or Germany or England, it was not essential to those countries. But to Japan, export markets meant food for her people — and as those people multiplied, ever-larger market areas had to be sought. Since this was a problem faced by leaders but one generation removed from a warrior-dominated feudal society — leaders who were themselves the inheritors of a still-vivid nationalism reinforced by the state religion and whose society was still permeated by the codes of military virtue — there was but little doubt that they would not hesitate to seek military solutions to the problem.

Japan's next opportunity to expand came with the outbreak of World War I in Europe. As the ally of Great Britain, Japan immediately declared war upon imperial Germany. Within months, the German-leased territory in China had fallen into Japanese hands and, of greater importance, so too had the German-owned island groups — the Carolines, Marshalls, and Marianas. With the acquisition of these island chains, Japanese power for the first time expanded into the central Pacific — there, eventually, to confront the American power based at Hawaii.

Since the European nations (and, after April 1917, the United States) were plunged up to their ears in the bloody war raging in Europe, Japan now undertook to carve out new economic spheres of influence in China. That unhappy country had been going through a time of revolution and civil war; the Manchu dynasty had been overthrown and, for a while, the revolutionary republican forces of Dr. Sun Yat Sen seemed dominant. But the real power in China soon reverted to local warlords; the entire nation was in chaos. Japan seized her opportunity and forced upon the prostrate Chinese a list of concessions known as the "Twenty-One Demands." Although not all were accepted,

Japan was granted the former German territory it then occupied, control of southern Manchuria, and many special privileges in Chinese commerce and industry.

The outbreak of the Russian Revolution in 1917 brought further opportunity to Japan. On the excuse of preserving allied war materiel piled high at Vladivostock and other Russian ports, Japanese and American troops occupied parts of Far Eastern Siberia where they encouraged and protected the establishment of anti-Communist regimes. It was quite probable that Japan was considering the annexation of some portion of Russia's Siberian and maritime provinces, but the presence of American troops restrained them (Lenin's Communist government privately thanked the United States government for its help), and Japanese forces were completely withdrawn a few years after World War I came to an end.

As the decade of the 1920s dawned, it had become apparent that there were now only two real Pacific powers — Japan and the United States. France still retained her colony of Indochina, but she had been bled white by World War I. England's fleet was still mistress of the seas, but the war had sapped her economic vitality to the point where it was questionable how much longer she could support the drain of imperial pretensions. Russia was wracked by revolution and so was China; both nations were far too concerned with domestic affairs to exert pressure outward. And, although it was not apparent at the time, the centuries-long dominance of the white man in Asia was also coming to an end. Revolutionary movements in all the European colonies were preparing to dispute their white masters. And many of these movements, though partly inspired by Russian communism, pointed eagerly to the Japanese example of an Oriental country that had not only modernized and saved itself from Western imperialism, but was even accepted as a great power on equal terms with the West. It was, perhaps, too soon for many Asiatics to realize that an Oriental nation could be fully as imperialistic and as racist-minded as any other.

From either side of the wide Pacific, then, Japan and the United States confronted each other. The question was whether a Pacific balance of power could be established peacefully between them; what role each would play in the unfolding drama of Asia's stormy awakening. For twenty years both countries sought an answer to this central problem. Their failure led to war.

The Road to War

The first attempt by the United States and Japan to establish an agreeable balance of power in the Pacific was the Washington Disarmament Conference of 1921–22. This meeting, attended by representatives of Great Britain, France, Japan, the United States, Italy, and lesser naval powers, was notable for the fact that Japan appeared more than willing to meet American demands.

The Japanese delegation agreed that Japan would limit the number of battleships and battle cruisers she built to 60 percent of those permitted to Britain or the United States; she agreed to return the German territory of Shantung to Chinese administration; she undertook to withdraw the last of her troops from the Soviet Far East; she reiterated her promise (made when Japan joined the League of Nations after World War I) that the former German central Pacific island chains, now held by Japan under League of Nations mandate, would not be fortified. And, of prime importance to both Japanese and American leaders, the Japanese-British Treaty of Alliance was to be replaced by a Four Power Treaty between Japan, France, Britain, and the United States the terms of which provided that all the powers agreed to cease fortifying their Pacific possessions and to maintain order over the entire region.

Advantageous as the terms of the Washington agreement seemed, they masked certain harsh realities. Firstly, Japan did not possess 60 percent as many battleships or battle cruisers as either England or the United States. Indeed, it would take her more than a few years to build up to this point, so its concession was meaningless. Secondly, both Japan and Britain already possessed important fortified bases in the Far East and Japan was busily fortifying certain of the mandated islands. But the United States, aside from the base at Cavite in the Philippines, had no Far Eastern fortifications worth mentioning. Thirdly, the Japanese-British Alliance was one that no English government had any intention of invoking against the United States — and as far as Japan was concerned there was no other potential enemy in the Pacific. Like so many treaties, that which emerged from the Washington Conference of 1922 was a recognition of the status quo and a pious wish that it might continue, not a resolution of real problems.

In the year following the Washington Conference, a great natural disaster exposed the flimsy structure of both the Japanese economy and its democratic political institutions. The disaster was the great earthquake of September 1, 1923. Untold thousands perished in this catastrophe and very large areas of Tokyo were flattened. The earthquake was followed by a fire storm that ravaged the rest of the nation's capital. Since much of Japan's industry was carried on by families doing piecework at home, the entire national economy suffered a blow from which it took years to recover. On December 27, a political fanatic attempted to assassinate the prince regent, Hirohito (grandson of the Emperor Meiji who had died in 1912), and thereby forced the resignation of the entire Japanese cabinet.

The United States, as well as other nations, rushed relief .supplies and help to the victims of the Tokyo earthquake. What-

View of Tokyo (above) shows the devastation wrought by the savage earthquake of September 1923. Photo below shows the same area exactly four years later, indicating how the enterprising Japanese had recouped from the tragedy.

ever good will was thus gained was wiped out when, in 1924, the United States Congress passed a new immigration act that absolutely barred any and all Asiatics. The Japanese, who had sincerely lived up to the Gentleman's Agreement reached with Theodore Roosevelt years before, were bitterly resentful of this blatantly racist discrimination.

But the real dividing line in Japan's attitude toward the rest of the world seems to have come as a result of the Great Depression. This worldwide economic collapse struck as hard in Japan as elsewhere; and, bearing in mind Japan's absolute necessity to export or die, it had consequences for Japan's international and domestic political life far greater than those experienced by other nations.

The depression struck most harshly against Japan's farmers and silkworm cultivators and, as agriculturists tend to do, they turned to extreme right-wing political groups to seek relief. These right-wing groups were inflamed by the superpatriotism that stemmed from the ancient samurai warrior traditions, and they were dominated by younger army and navy officers. Their solution to Japan's economic problems was to expand into the Asiatic mainland, thereby assuring a source of raw materials (including food), a place into which Japan's ever-burgeoning population might emigrate, and a captive market for Japanese manufactured products. Their program to win support for these ends was simple: they would assassinate any governmental, social, or economic leaders who opposed them. So effective was the terror they inspired in Japan's shaky parliamentary system that after 1932 most Japanese statesmen and politicians did not dare to oppose them.

A classical example of how the Japanese government was dominated by the military and by right-wing political organiza-

Victorious Japanese troops in Manchuria in 1931.

tions came in 1931. The Japanese forces in Manchuria (the Kwantung Army) had always enjoyed a semiautonomous position. In September 1931, the officers of the Kwantung Army, claiming that the railroad had been attacked by Chinese units stationed in Manchuria, and without consulting the Tokyo government, launched large-scale operations that drove Chinese troops from Manchurian soil. Not only was the Japanese government unable to control its forces in Manchuria, but the following year it also timidly agreed to the Kwantung Army's setting up a puppet state over the entire region to be known henceforth as "Manchukuo."

Many Japanese leaders realized that continued expansionism into Manchuria might well lead to war with China, and eventually perhaps to war with the United States. In fact, American Secretary of State Henry L. Stimson protested strongly to the Japanese and attempted to win English and French support for harsh measures against Japan. The most that could be done, however, was the issuance of a League of Nations report condemning Japan's aggression. But the military extremists in Tokyo found even this mild "wrist-slapping" too offensive; in 1933 Japan withdrew from the League of Nations.

In 1933, the Kwantung Army acted once again. It extended its control to parts of Inner Mongolia and set up a warlord-led puppet state embracing several districts of North China. Once again, the apprehensive Tokyo politicians had to accede to the Army's action. What could happen if they did not submit to the military will was vividly demonstrated in February 1936 when more than 1,500 Army officers and soldiers, alarmed by the fact that too many moderates had won office in the elections held that month, staged a bloody mutiny in which several high-ranking cabinet members were murdered. While the mutiny was suppressed, it was still apparent that the desperate spirit behind it enjoyed the support of many of the top military leaders and almost all the Army's junior officers. As if to underline the similarity between the philosophy of Japan's military extremists and the rising ideologies of German Nazism and Italian Fascism, Japan in 1936 joined Germany in an Anti-Commintern (anti-Communist) Pact clearly aimed against the Soviet Union; in 1937, Italy also joined.

In July 1937, Japan's militarists again seized the initiative. Taking advantage of a minor incident between small groups of men stationed outside Peking, the Japanese army and navy launched a full-scale attack against China. The great Chinese cities of Peking, Shanghai, Nanking, and Hankow were soon captured, after which Japanese armies spread their occupation deep into the interior. Although Japan continued to maintain that its actions were of a police nature, that nation did not declare war and always referred to the campaign in China as "the China incident." Even so, it was clear to the world that Japan was engaged in all-out war. And this in turn helped to consolidate the grip of the militarists upon the Japanese government.

Japan's invasion of China (accompanied by appalling brutalities to Chinese civilians) aroused great public resentment in the United States — and helped to convince American political and military leaders that war between the two nations was all but inevitable. When, during their campaign in China, Japanese planes sank the United States river gunboat *Panay* in December 1937, the resulting crisis was only partially cooled by Japanese apologies and reparations.

The U.S. gunboat Panay *sinking in the Yangtse River, December 1937.*

When World War II broke out in Europe the following year, Japan's militarists and a very large percentage of her people found themselves in sympathy with Hitler's Germany. And, after the Nazi conquest of France, Holland, and Belgium in the spring of 1940 — when it appeared that England would never be able to hold out against the German war machine — Japan's military leaders felt the time had come to take advantage of the situation. French, Dutch, and British power was now all but nonexistent in the Far East. If the Japanese dream of forcibly establishing a "Greater East Asia Co-Prosperity Sphere" (that is to say, seizing control of all the resources of the Far East) was ever to come true, this seemed the appropriate moment.

However, for Japan to prepare for the opportunities ahead, all political parties were dissolved in 1940 and replaced by the militarist-dominated Imperial Rule Assistance Association. Thus Japanese industry was placed under direct government control and Japan was swiftly transformed into a totalitarian state.

The first step in Japan's program of expansion was to conclude the endless war in China. To do this, it would be necessary to cut off the trickle of American and British aid that had been reaching the Chinese by way of British Burma and French Indochina. Accordingly, such strong pressure was placed upon Great Britain that the supply lifeline of the Burma Road was closed for three months. At the same time, the French were forced to allow Japanese troops to occupy northern Indochina.

If there was any doubt left as to Japan's territorial intentions, it was dispelled when Japan concluded a treaty of neutrality with her old Far Eastern enemy, Soviet Russia. Obviously Japanese leaders wanted to protect their flank while they attacked to the south. This intention was confirmed on July 29, 1941, when

With the signing of the Tripartite Pact in 1940, Emperor Hirohito's Japan joined its destinies with those of Adolf Hitler's Germany and Benito Mussolini's Italy.

63

Japanese troops occupied the whole of French Indochina; their mission could not be the sealing off of the already controlled northern border with China, it could only signal further expansion into Southeast Asia.

In actuality, the Japanese government had reached several basic decisions. It had decided that the future belonged (in Europe) to Hitler's Germany, and so it had, in September 1940, formally joined the German-Italian alliance (or Tripartite Pact). It had also decided that neither England nor any other European power would be able to defend itself in the Far East. It felt, therefore, that the United States could be intimidated into accepting Japanese expansion.

But the United States had not been an idle spectator of these events. The American government was well aware of the threat posed by European fascism in alliance with Japanese militarism. While the American Armed Forces were still too deplorably weak to intervene either in Asia or Europe, the nation was being converted into what President Roosevelt termed "the arsenal of democracy." Obviously, too, it was taking giant strides to prepare for a now inevitable conflict. In the meantime, to discourage further Japanese aggression, on July 26, 1941, the American government "froze" all Japanese assets in the United States and declared a total embargo on the sale of petroleum to Japan.

This action created a crisis. Japanese industry depended upon American petroleum and the petroleum of the Dutch East

Vanguard of President Roosevelt's "arsenal of democracy" was the U.S. Navy — the "first line of defense." Here the mighty battleship U.S.S. Arizona of the U.S. Pacific Fleet plows through heavy seas during exercises off Hawaii. A few months later it would be a twisted, blackened hulk off Ford Island at Pearl Harbor.

An aerial photo of the naval base at Pearl Harbor about one month before the Japanese attack.

66

Indies. When the Dutch government joined the United States in refusing to sell any more petroleum to Japan, the Japanese government was faced with a drastic choice. Since Japan's oil reserves were not great, it would have to conclude an agreement with the United States before those oil reserves were so depleted that the Japanese navy was immobilized. Without her Imperial Navy, Japan could not hope to conquer the very oil upon which her fleet depended. Japan's military and naval leaders were unanimous upon this vital point: if negotiations failed, war would have to be made before lack of supplies made war impossible. A date in late November 1941 was set as the absolute deadline beyond which Japan could not wait.

But negotiations with the United States (now undertaken by the Japanese government) always foundered upon the same points. The Americans insisted that Japan withdraw not only from French Indochina but also from China. However, after all the lives and funds expended in that continuing war, no Japanese leader could consider such a withdrawal; if he had, he would soon have been murdered by the militarists. In their turn, the Japanese demanded that the United States reopen trade, guarantee the sale of American petroleum products, accept the Japanese occupation of certain areas of China, and cease sending aid to the beleagured Chinese. But with war clouds gathering, no American government could possibly surrender on any of these points; to do so would simply be to enhance Japan's war-making capacity and prestige.

Thus, by mid-November 1941, it was apparent to Japanese leaders that no satisfactory arrangement could be reached with the United States. The deadline for action was approaching, but Japan's representatives in Washington, Admiral Nomura and

Special Envoy Kurusu, were encouraged to keep talking to American officials. This was necessary to gain time for the unfolding of a plan of attack that had been worked out many months before. The central blow in this plan was to be — like the one that opened the Russo-Japanese War in 1904 — a surprise attack on the enemy fleet.

That strike would be made by a large naval task force code-named *Kido Butai*. And, its bomb- and torpedo-laden planes would attack the United States Pacific Fleet anchored at Pearl Harbor in Hawaii just after dawn on December 7, 1941.

This captured Japanese photograph was taken by an enemy pilot during the first minutes of the attack. "Battleship row," with the great "battlewagons" still afloat, can be seen off the eastern tip of Ford Island.

Epilogue:
Sunset in the Pacific

The Japanese attack on Pearl Harbor was an overwhelming success. Unaware, unprepared, in the grip of peacetime habits and also of idiotic notions of the "inferiority" of all Orientals, the United States Pacific Fleet was all but destroyed by the well-planned, well-timed, and well-executed blow delivered against it that Sunday morning. Only the Pacific Fleet's aircraft carriers, not present in Pearl Harbor, escaped. Thus, the Japanese thought that American naval power in the Pacific had been neutralized for the indefinite future.

In the days and weeks following Pearl Harbor, the Japanese also successfully launched their fleets and armies against British Malaya (those two great battleships, the *Prince of Wales* and the *Repulse,* died within hours after a torpedo attack by the Japanese), against Hong Kong (which would capitulate in a matter of days), against the Philippine Islands (where they caught General Brereton's air force on the ground after all), and southward against the Dutch East Indies and to the waters above Australia.

So, while such great battleships of the United States Pacific Fleet as the proud *Arizona* and *Oklahoma* rusted beneath the waters of Pearl Harbor, no reinforcements could be sent to the Far East. Nor, as yet, could the United States Navy dispute control of Far Eastern waters with the Imperial Fleet. Likewise American, British, and Dutch air power was all-but-nonexistent in the Orient. With complete control of air and sea, the Japanese forces were able to carve out a huge empire extending from the borders of India to the waters of Hawaii, from the Aleutian Islands to the Coral Sea in a matter of six brief months. Now,

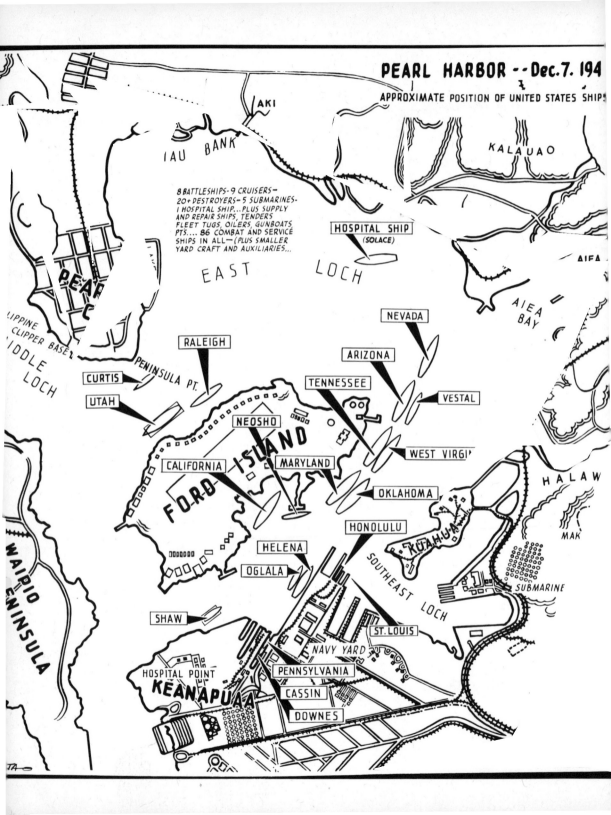

with the captured resources of this vast area, Japan would be, for the first time, economically self-sufficient. But for the empire of Japan the question was: Could this new empire be held?

Japanese leaders were not under many illusions regarding the potential strength of their chief adversary, the United States. They were well informed about America's gigantic industrial capacity. They also realized that sooner or later the fleet sunk at Pearl Harbor would be replaced. But they were engaged in a desperate gamble. They hoped that American attention would be diverted to Europe (Germany and Italy had declared war against the United States three days after Japan had) — and in this they proved to be correct. Recognizing that the German war machine was the greater threat, most American resources poured into the European theater of operations. Japanese leaders, hoped, too, that by seizing the outer island chains that formed

An American machine-gun crew in action against the Japanese attackers.

Above, a fireboat pours water on the burning U.S.S. West Virginia *after the attack. Below, a photographer's camera caught this spectacular explosion of the destroyer U.S.S.* Shaw *off the southern tip of Ford Island.*

Ruins of the once mighty American battlewagons are evident in this photograph taken shortly after the attack. In the foreground (from right to left): the U.S.S. Arizona in a sinking condition; behind her are the old cage masts of the U.S.S. Tennessee and U.S.S. West Virginia.

After the attack. Above, Ford Island in this aerial photo shows wreckage of great warships along "battleship row." Below, a B-17C bomber lies useless minus its tail section and midships fuselage on Hickam Field.

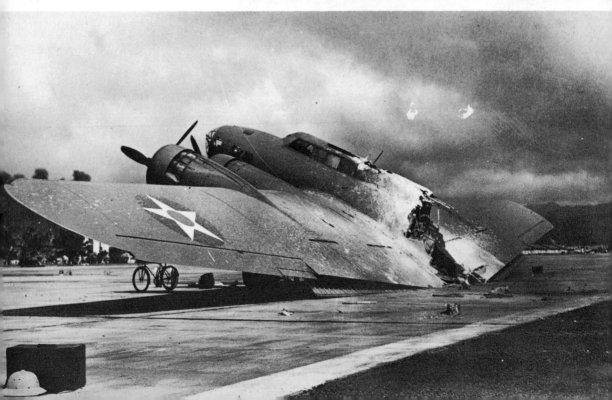

a natural barrier across the southern and central Pacific, they could establish "unsinkable" land-based air power that could hold at bay any new American fleet. Moreover they hoped that, faced with the appalling prospect of reconquering thousands of such islands against desperate resistance, the Americans would eventually weary of the struggle and sign a peace treaty that would enable Japan to retain some of its conquests.

The Japanese were wrong, of course. Even though most American resources went to the fighting in Europe, there were still enough left over to carry on extensive operations against Japan. Not one, but several, new American fleets made their appearance in the Pacific before the war was even two years old. These fleets, based on aircraft-carrier task forces, were so powerful that their planes could dominate the skies even over land. And the American people, infuriated by the Pearl Harbor attack, displayed no weariness whatsoever in pressing the fighting against island base after island base to the very doorstep of Japan.

As the bombers of *Kido Butai* roared down their carrier decks that Sunday morning, much lay behind them. There were the long years of fruitless attempts to establish peace in the Pacific. There were the decades during which Japan had, by her own efforts, launched herself as a great power in the modern world. And there was, behind them, the spirit of a feudal warrior nation.

Ahead of the attacking Japanese lay momentary triumph and then endless disaster. Ahead lay the great naval battles of the Coral Sea, Midway, Guadalcanal, and Leyte Gulf in which the Japanese Imperial Navy was utterly destroyed.

Ahead, too, lay the desperate fighting for such islands as Saipan, Iwo Jima, Tarawa, and Okinawa in which Japanese

Twilight of Japanese naval power in World War II is evident in these photos taken in 1944. Left, a battleship of the Yamato *class reels under attack by U.S. carrier aircraft off Japanese home islands. Above, Navy personnel cheering as enemy Kamikazi (suicide) plane hits the water ablaze during the Saipan and Tinian campaign.*

garrisons were obliterated almost to the last man. And ahead lay the destruction of Japanese cities by American fire-bombing and the ultimate horror of the atomic holocaust of Hiroshima and Nagasaki. Indeed, ahead lay total defeat for Japan.

Tokyo Bay, Japan, September 2, 1945. Fleet Admiral Chester Nimitz signs the Japanese surrender document aboard the battleship U.S.S. Missouri. Looking on (from left) are General Douglas MacArthur, Admiral William F. ("Bull") Halsey, and Admiral Forrest Sherman.

Yet just a little further in the future lay an American occupation of their native land that would bring greater transformations to Japanese life than all its history had yet shown. Ahead lay the destruction of Japanese militarism, the more equitable distribution of Japanese wealth, the firmer reestablishment of democratic government. Ahead, too, lay Japan's reacceptance in the international community, her friendship with the United States, and her emergence as one of the world's strongest and most prosperous economic powers.

The savage sunrise that dawned on December 7, 1941, ended in the sunset of Japanese power in the Pacific when Japanese delegates signed an unconditional surrender aboard the United States battleship *Missouri* in Tokyo Bay on September 2, 1945. Even so, a defeated Japan could look, as she had done for thousands of years, eastward across the vast Pacific to a new dawn.

The suns sets over Mount Fujiyama and Tokyo Bay on the day of surrender, September 2, 1945.

Chronology

c. 660 B.C. — Jimmu Tenno, descendant of the Sun Goddess, becomes the first emperor of Japan.

c. 700 A.D. — Chinese is adopted as the official language of Japan.

c. 850 A.D. — Sakanoue Tamuramaro becomes the first shogun in Japan.

1281 A.D. — A Mongol invasion of Japan is defeated.

1542 A.D. — The Portuguese discover Japan.

1549 A.D. — Francis Xavier introduces Catholicism to Japan.

1600 A.D. — Dutch merchants commence trade with Japan.

1637 A.D. — Japanese Christians are massacred, Japan is "closed" to the outside world.

1846 A.D. — American Commodore James Biddle unsuccessfully attempts to establish relations with Japan.

1854 A.D. — American Commodore Matthew C. Perry wrings a commercial and diplomatic treaty from the reluctant Japanese.

1859–60 A.D. — France and England negotiate treaties with Japan based on the American model.

1864 A.D. — British, French, Dutch, and American warships bombard the Japanese town of Shimonoseki.

1867 A.D. — The emperor Meiji ascends the Japanese throne; the shogunate is abolished a year later, and an era of reform and modernization begins.

1877 A.D. — The Satsuma Rebellion is suppressed.

1889 A.D. — First national constitution is promulgated.

1895 A.D. — Japan defeats the Chinese empire in war, wins control of Korea.

1898 A.D. — The United States wins the Philippine Islands from Spain and thereby becomes a Far Eastern power.

1904 A.D. — Japan defeats tsarist Russia in war, wins control of southern Manchuria.

1906 A.D. — California allows discriminatory laws against Japanese residents.

1908 A.D. — The American "Great White Fleet" visits Tokyo.

1910 A.D. — Japan annexes Korea outright.

1914–18 A.D. — Japan wins German territory in China and the Pacific and forces "Twenty-One Demands" upon strife-torn China.

1921–22 A.D. — Washington Disarmament Conference attempts to establish a balance of power in the Pacific.

1923 A.D. — Great earthquake devastates Tokyo.

1924 A.D. — United States Congress passes Asiatic Exclusion Immigration Act.

1931 A.D. — Japan's Kwantung Army seizes all of Manchuria.

1933 A.D. — Japan withdraws from the League of Nations.

1933 A.D. — Japan's Kwantung Army seizes certain areas of northern China.

1937 A.D. — Japan opens full-scale war against China.

1937 A.D. — Japanese planes sink United States gunboat *Panay* in Chinese waters.

1940 A.D. — All political parties in Japan are suppressed. Japan joins Hitler's Germany and Mussolini's Italy in the Tripartite Pact.

July 26, 1941 A.D. — United States places an embargo on trade with Japan.

July 29, 1941 A.D. — Japanese forces occupy French Indochina.

August–November 1941 A.D. — Japan and the United States negotiate to resolve differences.

December 7, 1941 A.D. — Japan unleashes war in the Pacific.

September 2, 1945 A.D. — Japan surrenders unconditionally.

Suggested Reading

Feis, Herbert. *The Road to Pearl Harbor*. Princeton, 1950.

Grew, Joseph C. *Ten Years in Japan*. New York, 1944.

James, David H. *The Rise and Fall of the Japanese Empire*. London, 1951.

Neumann, William L. *America Encounters Japan*. Baltimore, 1963.

Reischauer, Edwin O. *Japan Past and Present*. New York, 1964.

Sherwood, Robert E. *Roosevelt and Hopkins*. New York, 1948.

Togo, Shigenori. *The Cause of Japan*. New York, 1956.

Toland, John. *The Rising Sun*. New York, 1970.

White, Theodore H. *Thunder out of China*. New York, 1946.

Yanaga, Chitoshi. *Japanese People and Politics*. New York, 1956.

Index

86

About the Author

A native New Yorker and a graduate of Columbia University, Robert Goldston is the author of over thirty books for children and four adult novels. Now living and writing in Ibiza, Balearic Islands, his literary interests include such subjects as Spain and its many upheavals, the Russian and French revolutions, and the history of the Far East. In addition to *Pearl Harbor, The Long March, The Fall of the Winter Palace,* and *The Siege of the Alcazar,* Mr. Goldston plans to write several more World Focus Books for Franklin Watts, Inc.